Growing through Grief

Growing through Grief

by James E. Towns, Ph. D.

Warner Press
Anderson, Indiana
Arlo F. Newell, Editor in Chief

All scripture quotations, unless otherwise indicated are taken from The Holy Bible: Revised Standard Version of King James Version.

Warner Press, Inc.
1200 East Fifth Street
Anderson, IN   46011   USA

THIS GIFT
IS PRESENTED TO:

_____

With the deep hope that our
working together can
help you in the
healing process
of growing through your grief.

FROM:

_____

Contents

Acknowledgements

Preface

Chapter

1. WHY?!
   Laws of Nature • Human Imperfection •
   Community Living • Divine Impartiality
2. Normal Grief Process
   Shock• Emotion • Panic • Depression •
   Physical Distress • Guilt • Repression •
   Resentment • Hope—Acceptance
3. Scriptural Perspective on Grief
   Strength • Peace • Comfort • Position
4. Questions About Death Situations
   What basic knowledge should I have con-
   cerning what to do when a death occurs •
   Can someone help me get my business affairs
   in proper order • What can I say to someone
   in grief • How do I tell children about death

9

● What is the difference in the way a Christian and non-Christian meet death ● How can I prepare for my own death ● Where can I find help in the Bible when I have a time of need ●

Conclusion

Definition of Terms

Suggested Reading

GROW (gro), v. 1. spring up and come to maturity; 2. pass by degrees into a state or condition; come to be.

THROUGH (throo), prep. 1. during: from beginning to end; 2. because of.

GRIEF (gref), n. 1. deep sadness; 2. heavy sorrow resulting from loss.

Acknowledgments

No one ever writes a book alone, regardless of what the title page may assert. It is not possible in syllable and in sentence for me to express adequately my appreciation for the influence and concern of the many people who have encouraged me in this work.

I am indebted to the prayer warriors who consistently prayed for me while I was writing; and to the individuals with whom I have come in contact whose ideas have slipped unconsciously into my life-style—perhaps to have surfaced here as my own.

Special appreciation is expressed to Warner Press for their assistance in presenting these ideas.

Dedication

This book is presented
in
Gratitude to God for his love and grace
in
appreciation to my family and friends
for their understanding
and in
memory of a lovely lady who
lived for others,
and paid the price for my
knowledge concerning grief:
my mother
Mona Hancock Towns

Preface

THIS book had to be written! I have been deeply acquainted with death and grief. In a short span of time, I lost several family members and friends. Students in my classes at the university are sometimes absent due to a death in their family or friends. When they return to campus, they usually desire to talk with someone who cares. Many times they want to read a book that will assist them in coping with grief.

Probably no other single event is as life changing as the death of someone you deeply loved! In my early grief, I treated my thoughts and feelings as if they were abnormal. Soon I learned that regardless of how strong a Christian faith a person has, it is normal to have disturbing feelings during the process of grief. As I began to understand sorrow, I tried to help bereaved people to profit from my new insights. Each time I go to be with a family in fresh sorrow, I want to be able to present them with a brief power-packed book that will help them to understand their normal grief behavior. This is why this book had to be written. It is for those who are in grief and those who need to understand sorrow in order to help a relative or friend.

Writers have always had difficulty using the confining tool of words to describe ideas, attitudes, and concepts. My purpose is to attempt to put in words some helpful hints from the Christian perspective concerning how to communicate effectively with yourself and others about the normal grief process.

This book is written for those who personify Mark 9:24, "I believe, help my unbelief." It is designed to try to explain the logic of the Christian faith concerning death.

Many times when a tragedy occurs, people tend to blame God harshly for what has happened. This book presents the scriptural perspective of the human being as a free moral agent interacting with God's natural law and sovereignty. It is a practical statement about how to respond in the process of normal grief

Take a look at grief. If you have known it, you will remember. If you have not lost someone you love, then imagine yourself suddenly alone in an alien world. Your body is weary, your emotions are raw. Your heartache is a real physical ache. You are convinced that your life is destroyed. You do not know how to think, how to stop feeling, how to start feeling, what to do and what not to do. Knowledge cannot erase our emotions that accompany sorrow, but knowledge can help us guide ourselves and each other toward recovery.

Our contemporary society has no time for death. A death is usually handled quickly and rapidly forgotten by most people. Yet grief remains. The great complicated task is how to accept the breakup of family unity and function under the high pressure and fast pace of life today in such a way that grief does not destroy the survivors.

This book is about adjustment. It is not a complex theological or philosophical work, but a simple direct statement of what behavior is like when a person is in bereavement.

People can search in several places for answers to grief: philosophy, psychology, sociology, and science. Please do not misunderstand; All these are good if they are used appropriately. However, if I am honest, I must use my intellectual integrity and give the Christian faith an opportunity to work in my life. Readers are free to accept or reject some behavior principles based on God's Word. This book is launched with the prayer that many may learn to treat their normal grief behavior in a normal way.

If these ideas stimulate questions and discussion and provide some answers, they will have served a meaningful purpose. If you will think, plan, and prepare to accept grief and sorrow as a part of life, perhaps you will avoid the dangerous trend of treating your normal grief behavior as if it were abnormal.

Jim Towns
Department of Communication
Stephen F. Austin State University
Nacogdoches, Texas

Chapter 1:
Why?!

DEATH is the strongest force known to most people. Paul Tillich pointed out that every person always lives in the conscious or unconscious anxiety of having to die. Death may come at any time. There is never a time when we should be surprised, yet there seldom seems to be a right time for dying.

The subject of death is a taboo topic for many people. In spite of this, it is a matter of individual concern. Although most people do not want to talk about it, they do desire to know more about how to deal with the grief process.

When the death of a loved one occurs, most people go through a period of questioning their existence as well as questioning

God. In order to better understand life and death, we must blend reason and faith. Some people feel that it is rude to question God. It depends on whether the quest is an honest search in faith for meaning or whether it is a challenge of unbelief and rebellion.

The wrong kind of why usually does not call for an answer; it calls for an argument. We demand that we know the ultimate why. In our grief we want answers and comfort. We desire to know primarily why things happened. Ultimately, I have come to realize that God has a grand scheme of design, and I cannot figure out all the primary reasons for events happening as they do. God is sovereign in the design of life and death. The why of an honest search for answers is not the same as the rebellious, belligerent why. The right kind of questioning can bring about some comfort and relief in human understanding.

My first experience with death in my immediate family resulted in a lingering slow adjustment to a new normal life. If I had known then what I now know about the normal grief process, I would have mourned, of course, but I would have been aware of what was happening to me. I would have known how to respond to my bewildering emotions and what to expect from my normal psychological behavior. I had so many unanswered questions and feelings. It is normal to ask why.

At first I turned to logic to provide my answers for why the death happened. It is inevitable that all people die. I thought that if I could have reasons or purposes I could better accept my losses. This line of thinking yielded the idea that suffering and tragedy are not caused by gross and terrible sins that we have committed or simply by the judgmental will of God. God does not randomly and impersonally will tragedy on us. If we trust him, he is the God of love who is there to take care of us in all aspects of life and death. Many times we blame God for something that we possibly could have brought on ourselves.

Scripture teaches that sorrow and suffering in the world are many times the direct and indirect result of sin. The one word that best describes the consequences of sin is *death*. Sin is the breaking of God's law. In other words, it is anything that interferes with our having an adequate relationship with God through Jesus Christ.

Breaking God's law carries the death penalty. He said to Adam and Eve: "In the day that thou eatest thereof thou shalt surely die" (Gen. 2:17). Paul summed it up in these words: "The wages of sin is death" (Rom. 6:23).

There are two kinds of death. Both are the results of sin. Physical death is the transition or separation of body and spirit. This death results in the decay of the body (Eccles. 12:7). The death of the physical body is part of the penalty of sin. If there had not been any sin, there would have been no physical death. Adam and Eve would not have died had they not sinned. From that day to this, death has been in the world. The Christian will experience only physical death.

Spiritual death is the separation of the spirit from God. This death results in the ruin of the spirit. "Those who do not know God . . . shall suffer the punishment of eternal destruction and exclusion from the presence of the Lord and from the glory of his might" (2 Thess. 1:8-9). Just as spiritual birth is more glorious than physical birth, the spiritual death is more terrible than physical death.

Although there are no easy satisfying answers to the primary questions of why, there are some secondary principles that come from earnest searching.

The right kind of questioning can bring about some comfort for human understanding. Within God's love and sovereignty four major secondary variables interact. Humanity is subjected to these variables because of the direct or indirect result of the Fall of Man. These secondary variables are these: laws of nature, human imperfection, community living, and divine impartiality.

Laws of Nature

The laws of nature are natural indiscriminating laws. God set natural law into motion. The nature world has both assets—beauty, wealth, and the like—as well as liabilities—disease, tornados, floods, earthquakes, and the like.

Disease is one of the laws of nature. There are no simple answers for why some people contract diseases and others never seem to be sick. God does not make people get sick nor does he indiscriminately will disease on a person. If we blame God, then we have an inadequate theology or concept of who he is and how he works.

The material environment that God has

provided finds its stability in the fact that it is law-abiding. The rain may aid one set of human purposes and harm another. It may seem at times that the world and environment are cruel and hopeless, but there is a stability.

God does not always heal the diseased physical body. A Christian doctor related that he prays for healing—if it is God's will. He never tells patients that they will be physically healed if they have enough faith. People who say that God always heals if one has enough faith are often strangely inconsistent. They wear false teeth, glasses, and other artificial aids. In the Bible is a principle that could be called the "Economy of the Miraculous." God doesn't work a miracle when a normal way is available and he does not always intervene when the case is medically hopeless.

Human Imperfection

Humans have a frail framework. They cannot always see what is best or right in ultimate terms. People make decisions and must live with the consequences, whether good or bad Many times people blame God for accidents or mistakes. The real reasons often are due to human imperfection.

A plane crash in a storm may point out human imperfection in the decision-making processes. The pilot or his or her superiors saw the storm. They could have gone around it or over it or turned back. But they decided that it would be all right to go through it. But the raging storm was worse than they had anticipated. Something dreadful happened. No one knows for sure. The tragic plane crash came as a result of human imperfection in reasoning out what to do about the approaching storm.

Accidents are often a result of someone's imperfect reasoning. Many automobile accidents could have been avoided if the drivers had been responsible and considerate of one another. If automobiles go fast enough to provide needed transportation, they will also go fast enough to destroy lives.

Disease may result from imperfect reasoning. We reason that the food is delicious as we gorge ourselves. Perhaps elements in our diets react against the physical body, allowing diseases to find their beginnings. Some processed food products may not be healthful.

Perhaps we did not do the right thing at the right time in order to avoid becoming ill. We may not have sought proper medical attention at the proper time. It is our imperfect reasoning powers that get us into problems. Most of the time we are asking why God does not do something to help us in these matters, and he is probably wondering why we do not do more with our knowledge and ability.

Community Living

We do not live to ourselves in this world. As population explodes we realize that what one person does has an effect on others. When one person gets the flu, usually many people get it. Epidemics take their toll.

In 1966 a young man climbed to the top of the tower on the University of Texas campus. He pulled out a gun and began shooting students in all directions. Then the man shot himself. Because he lived in a community, Charles Whitman not only hurt himself with a gun at the University of Texas tower, he also hurt twenty-one other people. If Whitman had been on a deserted island it would have been a different story. But he was in a community of people and his actions hurt many innocent people. It seems senseless, but many times the actions of others bring harm or death to innocent bystanders.

In community living, tragedies may result if people are not responsible and considerate of one another. In our contemporary society the misuse of alcohol and drugs has taken an overwhelming toll in harming people. Many innocent people have been harmed by another person who is under the influence of drugs.

Divine Impartiality

Good comes to good people and bad people. Bad comes to good people and bad people. It rains on the just and the unjust.

Think about the example of the two houses and foundations of sand and rock (Matt. 7:24-27). The storms, rain, and wind came to both houses. They did not just come to the house on sand. The house on the rock stood—but it did go through the storm. If the foundation of a person's life is God's Word, he or she will be standing during and after the storm.

When I was in deep sorrow, going through a storm, doubts flooded my mind. At a major crisis point, I made the following statement of commitment:

As I walk the way of inquiry which has produced doubt, uncertainty, and rank skepticism, I'm not afraid to entrust an unknown immediate future to my known God.

So many things have happened that could make my actions be based on superstition, but I'm not afraid to entrust an unknown immediate future to my known God.

I've endeavored in many seemingly worthwhile activities but have produced few visible affirmative results, but I'm not afraid to entrust my unknown immediate future to my known God.

When I question why, I realize that God wants me to know. "My little child, if you could see it the way I see it, you would not worry, you would know that I am taking care of you in a very special way." I'm not afraid to entrust an unknown immediate future to my known God.

Later on, I became aware that the grumbling that I was doing toward the situation, and my unanswered questions were not against the situation; they were against God!

In the situations that occur in life, I feel that God must be thinking, I must be faithful to these humans. They are trusting themselves, friends, family, and society rather than me. People must trust me. To be sensible in life's situations is to be dependent on God. In order to understand and adjust, a Christian must think as God thinks. It is through his Word that we learn how he thinks. People must respond, "Thank you Lord; you are in charge" (See 1 Thess. 5:18.)

God is sovereign. The devil could not accuse people until God permitted him to do so. In Job 38-40, Job asked why all the sorrow and grief had come to him. He tried to tell God that there was a better way to do things. Job thought he was wise. Then God asked Job some questions that proved his providence and sovereignty. When Job realized who God was and more about his plans, he responded to God by saying, "I do not know everything. How could I ever find the answers? I lay my hand upon my mouth in silence. I have said too much already."

Some of the answers to my whys have been revealed in the fact that God dared to show me what a sinful man I am and what still lay in my subconscious. Because he trusted himself in me, he let the darkness or storm come. But he continued to work.

Rather than ask for answers to unanswerable questions, I can thank God for the life and work of the deceased.

Chapter 2:
Normal Grief Process

HUMAN grief is too complex for simplistic labels. Therefore, this is an attempt to describe steps or stages of normal grief. One of the major reasons that most people have trouble adjusting is that they do not understand the normal grief process. They treat their normal behavior as if it were very abnormal. This compounds problems. Many people do not understand adjustments simply because they have never been confronted with the issue. They never thought to prepare or to expend effort to understand the normal grief process.

Despite the inevitability of death, bereavement is usually unexpected and is accompanied by a process of grief.

No matter how brave and strong we are,

or think we can be, we must call grief or sorrow by its right name in order to comprehend it for what it is. We should not, by any reflection or twist of words we use, minimize what we are going through when death removes a member of our family or a friend. A fact remains: someone we loved is deceased; he or she is no longer with us. We are human and we miss the person.

Grief is the process through which we readjust to our environment in which the deceased is missing and start forming new relationships. In other words, it is a series of thoughts, feelings, and actions during a period of adjustment to the loss of a loved one. Most people are inadequate within themselves to cope with all the crisis situations surrounding death.

When death occurs, the survivor experiences several stages of grief. Each individual does not necessarily go through all the stages, nor does he or she necessarily go through the stages in the order in which they are presented here. Sometimes it is difficult to differentiate between each of the stages. The normal grief process may include shock, weeping, panic, depression, physical distress, guilt, resentment, repression, and hope.

Whether anticipated or unanticipated, the death of a loved one causes a person to go through a grief process of theological and/or philosophical adjustment to the loss. The predominantly theological person makes his or her adjustment by making the daily experience synonymous with his or her scriptural position in Christ. For the predominantly philosophical person, the tendency is to be dependent on humanistic solutions and rationalization.

Shock

Shock is a blow, impact, or sudden agitation of the mental or emotional sensibilities. It is a numbing reaction we may experience immediately upon hearing about the death of someone we love.

Shock may last a few minutes, hours, or days. If it goes on for weeks, it becomes unhealthy. Do not be afraid of the shock that occurs at first. On several occasions when I have learned of the death of someone dear to me, I have been stunned. I walked around in almost a trance or daze. I heard people talking to me, but the words did not register. I was numb.

Shock is a temporary escape from reality. Shock is also the body's natural way of

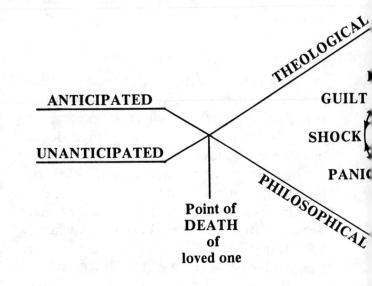

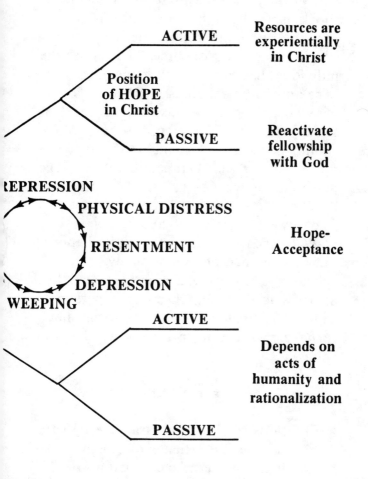

ACTIVE — Resources are experientially in Christ

Position of HOPE in Christ

PASSIVE — Reactivate fellowship with God

REPRESSION

PHYSICAL DISTRESS

RESENTMENT

Hope-Acceptance

DEPRESSION

WEEPING

ACTIVE

Depends on acts of humanity and rationalization

PASSIVE

protection and God's provision or gift to endure grief for a while. After a few hours or days we must face the reality of the loss. One of the best things to do for someone in shock is to keep him or her fairly busy carrying on as much usual activity as possible during this crisis time. The sooner the individual has to deal with immediate problems and make decisions, the better. Otherwise he or she could lose a great deal of self-confidence and contact with reality. We should be near and available to help, but not to hinder the therapeutic value of the person doing what he or she is able to do.

When in a state of shock I sometimes find myself saying, "I cannot believe this really happened." I know that it did happen, but I cannot accept it emotionally.

There is not only a mental shock, but also a social shock. A married person is suddenly a single person. It is a social shock to have to function in society without the spouse.

Emotion

Emotions cannot be separated from situations or experiences that evoke them. Emotion is an inside thermometer that is affected by outside events. When a person is in grief, weeping is an impulse toward expressing actions that come from inner feelings. The first step in dealing with weeping is to realize the fact that it is an emotion and that it is God's way of helping us to relieve inner pressure.

Our emotions come when what we have lost begins to dawn upon us. For many people emotions well up with an uncontrollable urge to express their grief; this is normal. The most healthy thing to do is to allow ourselves to weep and express the emotions we actually feel.

In the American society it is difficult for some men to cry. They have been taught from the moment they put on their first pair of shoes that little boys do not cry. Therefore, many men think that weeping is a sign of weakness. If they tense up and refuse to express their emotions, they may be in for trouble.

I am not talking about emotionalism. One of the faults of many spiritual robots is that their perspective has tended to stifle the expression of sorrow upon the death of a loved one. We should encourage the expression of grief. Sometimes people are embarrassed to sorrow or weep openly. If this is the case, they should be by themselves and let their sorrow take its natural course. We can release our emotions in a number of ways but most of all, we should not keep them bottled up within ourselves. Express them to yourself, to a friend, or to someone whom you know cares for you. There is truth in the idea that a joy shared doubles it; a sorrow shared halves it. This may not be a once-for-all happening. It is normal to continue to weep at times about your loss for a year or two. Significant days concerning the deceased are hard to face—days such as birthdays, Mother's Day, or anniversaries.

Panic

Panic is a sudden, severe, overpowering fright. When we become confronted or obsessed with our loss, in some instances we become panicky because we can think of nothing but the loss. When I am in the grief process, it seems that my mind can go only a few seconds without thinking about my loss. The inability to concentrate is normal and natural during the grief process.

It is the fear of the unknown or fear of something that we do not understand that causes us to panic. Therefore, it is important that people understand something about the grief process in advance of their loss so that they will not treat this normal behavior as if it were abnormal. This kind of knowledge can eliminate part of the panic.

The first time I experienced the grief process and was in deep sorrow, I did not know what to expect. I thought that my life was a wreck because of the feelings that flooded me. I began to panic; I thought that I might even be losing my mind because I could not control my feelings, thoughts, and words.

Gloom soon surrounds panic. Often times it is natural to want to be alone. However, we must not linger in our gloom because this will extend our adjustment time. It is a comfort to understand that even panic is a normal reaction to a stressful situation as death. Panic may soon evolve into depression.

Depression

In the normal grief process many people may eventually feel depressed. Depression is the saddening and lowering of our mental spirit brought about by an extreme difficulty or burden. It is the emotional state of dejection or despair and feelings of worthlessness and apprehension.

When we find ourselves in the depth of depression or despair we begin to feel that no one has ever had a loss as significant as ours. Then something seems to come between us and our family, friends, and even God. When this happens we find ourselves thinking thoughts that we would never otherwise have ventured. At one point in my deep sorrow, I felt that no one cared. I knew that he could have kept the death from happening if he would have wanted, but he did not. And I was mad. It is easy to get a persecution complex when we are depressed.

Depression comes to most people when someone they love is taken away from them. One of the most beneficial things we can do for someone depressed in grief is to stand by him or her in quiet confidence and assure the person that "this too shall pass." The bereaved will probably not understand at first. As the length and intensity of the depression lessens, he or she has a fuller appreciation for those who are standing by.

For some people the depression clouds seem to roll away. For others it may take weeks and months before any new rays of light break through. If depression is prolonged it is highly possible that physical and mental distress will occur.

Physical Distress

Physical distress is the endurance of physical pain and symptoms of illness due to the grief process. Many people become physically ill because of an unresolved grief situation. They have not worked through the problems relating to the death. Unless somehow persons can resolve their emotional problems relative to the normal grief process, then they may possibly become physically ill. Notice I said resolve not solve. We must resolve ourselves into acceptance and adjustment.

One of the major causes of illness during the grief process is that "as [a man] thinketh, so is he" (Prov. 23:7). The hard, depressing emotions of a person's mind and personality can make his or her body physically sick. Some of the physical symptoms of distress during the grief process may be these: 1) feeling tightness in the throat, 2) choking with shortness of breath, 3) need for sighing, 4) empty feeling in the abdomen, 5) lack of muscular power, and 6) an intensive distress described as tension. When a person is in the grief process his or her night dream world may be plagued with horrible dreams about the situation or death of the deceased. These dreams may emotionally drain a person for hours or days. This kind of physical and mental distress is normal. When a person feels distress and sorrow, he or she may start feeling guilty about some of the factors in the grief process.

Guilt

Normal guilt is a feeling of having committed a breach of conduct. Guilt comes when one does not meet what persons expect of themselves as well as what others expect of them. Neurotic guilt is feeling guilty out of proportion to the real involvement in the particular problem.

Guilt feelings often come when we feel that we should have been there to do or to suggest something that may have been some comfort or assistance to the deceased.

Negative guilt feelings may come when we realize that we did not treat the deceased in the appropriate manner. First John 1:9 is a good prescription for guilt. If we confess,

God is faithful to forgive and cleanse. Negative guilt and misunderstood emotions make us miserable for a long time. We must not be afraid to talk about our feelings of guilt with those who care for us.

Often we feel that responsibility to the loved one has not been properly taken care of while the person was alive. Sometimes there is a basis for this, but on many occasions, this may not be true. Whatever the reason for feelings of guilt, it should be realized that it is normal to feel guilty because we could not make our situation better. When we cannot make the situation or conditions better, then resentment or repression occurs.

Repression

Repression is a defense behavior by which an individual prevents painful thoughts and desires from entering his or her conscious mind. In other words, it is selective forgetting. The thoughts are not really forgotten. They keep coming back to the conscious mind.

Repressed feelings continue to influence behavior. Oftentimes the person is unaware of the real basis for some of his or her thoughts, beliefs, and actions. A new painful experience may trigger a flood of may repressed feelings. If a person is trying to repress his or her feelings about the death of a loved one, and suddenly sees a funeral procession, he or she may break into tears. The person could not continue to repress the painful feelings that were bottled up inside.

Repressed feelings or thoughts may be very active and may find an outlet in dreams when the conscious mind lowers its controls. When a person is under continued frustration, repressed thoughts may increase in strength and threaten to break through into the conscious mind and even into overt actions.

Threats of mentally painful experiences lead to the arousal of anxiety and additional defenses. Repression takes considerable mental energy that is then not available for direct attempts to resolve the problems of life.

Many times when repressed feelings are allowed to come into the conscious mind, resentment may spring up. If resentment is not adequately treated immediately, then many problems may arise.

Resentment

Resentment is the feeling of indignant displeasure because of something regarded as wrong. In our depression, strong feelings of hostility and resentment may rise.

Many who are in the grief process go through a time of being very critical of everything and everyone who was related to the loss. As persons try to understand why the death happened, they tend to blame others. They express resentment to anyone who cared for the patient. No matter what was done on behalf of the deceased, they feel that it was insufficient.

This type of resentment gives rise to a question like, "Why did God let this happen?" Remember, there are laws of nature, human imperfection, community living, and divine impartiality. At times persons become so desperate in their resentment that they cannot live with themselves, much less with anyone else. Resentment hurts oneself more than anyone else.

It is comforting to know that all this behavior is normal in the grief process. In spite of resentment and all other emotions, there is hope.

Hope-Acceptance

Hope is the expectation toward obtaining a comfortable new normal life. We need to express our emotions. We need encouragement from others. Some people take an attitude of shutting out possibilities for a new and meaningful normal life. Notice that I did not say possibilities for the old and meaningful normal life again. The past is gone. Life will never again be the same as we knew it with our loved one. But there can be a new normal life.

When I experienced deep sorrow in the grief process for the first time, I felt that I would never be happy again. Nothing could ever ease the heartache. I did not know that it was normal to feel that way for a while. Hope lies only in acceptance. Hope and peace are not found in forgetting, in resignation, or in busyness. Acceptance is the key. You may ask, "But how do I accept something that I don't want to accept?" Are you willing to be willing to let go of your selfish motives and trust God in his sovereignty? If the answer is no, then keep praying for a willingness to be willing.

God is never weary with our new beginnings. Ask God for thoughts of mind and impressions of heart as you accept his ultimate sovereign plan for your life. The Bible is a record of people who have taken God at his word and trusted. God does not always grant us our wants, desires, and wishes, but he does meet our needs. Many times I get the definitions of these words mixed up. I think that a desire or wish or want is a need. I believe that God meets our real needs as we trust him. Jesus comes to us at the point of our need and shows that his Word will give us meaning and purpose in life.

People of faith do not suddenly get that way. The Christian grieves deeply over his or her loss and goes through the grief process. Eventually we understand that everything has not been taken from us and we want to live again.

Hope and reality are based on faith in God's Word. Though we continue to struggle, we do find a new normal life. The struggle is hard if we try to do it on our own. Relax and take God at his Word, regardless of how you feel.

In the next chapter we will become aware of what God's Word will do for us while we are in the grief process.

Chapter 3:
Scriptural Perspective on Grief

MY first experience in grief resulted in despair. Many people tried to help by giving me books to read. I was disillusioned with the standard books concerning death. Some friends even suggested that I read certain selected scriptures in the Bible. At one point my sorrow was so deep that I was tempted never to look at a Bible again because I was angry at God.

If you feel cold toward reading the Bible and this reflects your attitude also, then we can empathize through this chapter as I reveal that my inadequate concepts of God made me not want to read his Word. I was not willing to be willing to be open to God and let his Word change my perspective. An important question comes to you now. Are you willing to be willing to give God's Word a chance to change your heart and mind and give you the comfort that you need so desperately right now? Whether the answer is yes or no, I want to present a challenge. Start each day of your life with a brief prayer: "Lord Jesus, please make yourself better known to me. Fill my life. Take charge of it and use it as you see fit." If you really mean that prayer, some incredibly wonderful things will happen to you!

I discovered that the Bible reveals much about people who have had the same needs that I now have!

Perhaps by now you are thinking, It sounds good, but I have heard that kind of thing before and it always turns out to be the same old cold experience when I read the Bible. Let me assure you that I am aware of this problem. I suggest that you ask God to help you to reject your feelings and by faith take him at his Word. Mark 9:24 states it perfectly, "I believe; help my unbelief."

When I rejected my feelings and began to trust the Lord by faith, my reading the Bible changed my old perspective. I soon took the stand on which I now rest my case: I avowedly accept the Bible as the authoritative Word of God which presents the standard of faith and practice. It is the revelation of God's actions with his people throughout the ages, particularly through Jesus Christ.

The Bible contains the truths, prophecies, and a message of hope to the human race that could not have been the mere product of human minds. Truths are set forth in the scripture that human beings could never have known if these truths had not been divinely revealed. The fulfillment of prophecy bears witness to the inspiration of the Bible. The message of the scriptures attests its inspiration. It tells us the kind of God we have. It reveals the awful nature and consequence of sin. It points out the way of salvation and the real purpose of life.

These scriptures are presented with full assurance that God's Word will not return void, but will accomplish what he pleases in your life.

God's Promises Based on His Word

Keep in mind that, whether anticipated or unanticipated, the death of a loved one may cause both the Christian and non-Christian to go through a grief process in adjustment to the loss. The Christian makes his or her adjustment by making daily experience synonymous with his or her position in Christ. In other words, the Christian must make his or her daily routine activities and perspective consistent with Scripture.

When I was in the different stages of the grief process (shock, weeping, panic, depression, physical distress, guilt, resentment, and repression) I did not even try to employ God's Word in my routine daily life. I was too busy feeling sorry for myself concerning my loss. As I continued in a deep sadness, I began to despair. At this point I began to read the Bible.

When I became willing to be willing to be open to God's Word, I found out it really works! I felt so weak and inadequate. I needed strength.

Strength

Isaiah 40:28-30

Have you not known? Have you not heard? The Lord is the everlasting God, the Creator of the ends of the earth. He does not faint or grow weary, His understanding is unsearchable. He gives power to the faint, and to him who has no might he increases strength. Even youths shall faint and be weary, and young men shall fall exhausted; but they who wait for the Lord shall renew their strength, they shall mount up with wings like eagles, they shall run and not be weary, they shall walk and not faint.

2 Corinthians 12:9

My grace is sufficient for you, for my power is made perfect in weakness.

The more selfish I became during the grief process, the less peace I had in my life. Scripture gives explicit statements concerning how to obtain the peace that we need so desperately.

Peace

Romans 5:1-6

Therefore, since we are justified by faith, we have peace with God through our Lord Jesus Christ. Through him we have obtained access to this grace in which we stand, and we rejoice in our hope of sharing the glory of God.

Closely connected to the need for peace was the need for comfort.

Comfort

John 14:1-3

Let not your hearts be troubled; believe in God, believe also in me. In my Father's house are many rooms; if it were not so, would I have told you that I go to prepare a place for you? And when I go and prepare a place for you, I will come again and will take you to myself, that where I am you may be also. And you know the way where I am going.

As I started trusting God, I began to learn more about his loving kindness and grace. In God's grace, we are given a position with him.

Position

1 Thessalonians 4:13-18

But we would not have you ignorant, brethren, concerning those who fall asleep, that you may not grieve as others do who have no hope. For since we believe that Jesus died and rose again, even so, through Jesus, God will bring with him those who have fallen asleep. For this we declare to you by the word of the Lord, that we who are alive, who are left until the coming of the Lord, shall not precede those who have fallen asleep. For the Lord himself will descend from heaven with a cry of command, with the archangel's call, and with the sound of the trumpet of God. And the dead in Christ will rise first; then we who are alive, who are left, shall be caught up together with them in the clouds to meet the Lord in the air; and so we shall always be with the Lord. Therefore comfort one another with these words.

2 Corinthians 5:1-10

For we know that if the earthly tent we live in is destroyed, we have a building from God, a house not made with hands, eternal in the heavens. Here indeed we groan, and long to put on our heavenly dwelling, so that by putting it on we may not be found naked. For while we are still in this tent, we sigh with anxiety; not that we would be unclothed, but that we would be further clothed, so that what is mortal may be swallowed up by life. He who has prepared us for this very thing is God, who has given us the Spirit as a guarantee.

So we are always of good courage; we know that while we are at home in the body we are away from the Lord, for we walk by faith, not by sight. We are of good courage, and we would rather be away from the body and at home with the Lord. So whether we are at home or away, we make it our aim to please him. For we must all appear before the judgment seat of Christ, so that each one may receive good or evil, according to what he has done in the body.

Read and believe scripture. It tells you about the goodness of God and the immortality of the soul. As you trust the Bible, you will find a deep conviction welling up in your mind that his words are true indeed!

These have been selected scriptures concerning what God's Word says about death.

Chapter 4:
Questions about Death Situations

W HAT basic knowledge would I have concerning what to do when a death occurs? Whom should I call?

Sometime, a relative or friend may turn to you in time of bereavement. You will be faced with new and sudden responsibilities. You must take care of many unfamiliar things—at once! Any death creates an emergency situation for the family. In this emotional crisis you will probably need to contact these people to help make arrangements:

1. Attending physician or medical examiner. If a doctor was attending the deceased, he will help you start making arrangements. If

the death was the result of violence or could have been the result of a criminal act, the medical examiner must examine the circumstances. The police will help you with many details.

2. Funeral director. Contact a funeral director whom you respect. He or she will advise you and guide you in your selections. You should feel no embarrassment in discussing with the director your desires and ability to pay. The staff should be helpful in making suitable arrangements that are right for the family.

The funeral director should secure necessary burial permits and death certificates. He or she will counsel with you regarding the funeral plans, place obituary and funeral notices in the newspapers that you desire, and contact radio stations.

If the deceased is to be taken to a distant point for burial, the funeral director will make the necessary arrangements.

The funeral director's job is to assist you in every way to make the funeral a memorial service that is an expression of your faith.

3. The minister. The minister will offer comfort to the family and make himself or herself available to all who need special counseling. He or she will help you to set

up the order of the funeral service. Ask the minister to conduct a Christian memorial victory service based on God's Word rather than to conduct a sad funeral.

The minister will collaborate closely with the funeral director in planning the details of the service at the church and at the grave site.

4. Family and friends. You may need to call members of the family and close friends and inform them of the death that has occurred. Ask others to aid in making the many calls that must be made.

Feel free to ask others to help in meeting the needs of those in grief. Everyone close will want to express through word and deed that they care.

Who can help me get my business affairs in proper order?

Special Organizational Services, Inc. (SOS)* has been established to help meet this need.

About SOS

No one wants to think about it, but with

---

*Ideas and materials used by permission, Mr. Bill Walker, President, Special Organizational Services, Inc., Athens, Texas.

the death of a loved one, families are always confronted immediately with matters that must be taken care of in settling various business and personal affairs. In order to help families during this time of adjustment, many banks offer SOS services at no cost or obligation that can save survivors time and unnecessary confusion.

How SOS works

At time of need, family members are invited to call the SOS bank and arrange, at their convenience, for an appointment with one of the SOS advisors. Working with a member or members of the family, the advisor will prepare a comprehensive written checklist defining the proper authorities to be notified and where they are located, certain practical measures that should be taken, and the documents and other basic information that will be required in filing claims for such benefits as . . .

Social Security
Civil Service
Life Insurance
Pension Plans
Railroad Retirement
Profit Sharing Plans

Teacher's Benefits
Veteran's Benefit

Knowing the exact documents needed in filing various claims gives family members the opportunity to assemble data that is required and avoid repeated conferences with claims personnel at various government agencies.

ORGANIZATION CONSISTS OF:

(Pre-survivor)

(Post survivor)

What—documents need to be located or applied for.

Why —these documents are needed.

How —these documents are obtained.

What—documents are needed to file claims.

Why —these documents are needed.

How —benefits are obtained (using copyright checklist.)

DIRECTION CONSISTS OF:

(Pre-survivor)

(Post survivor)

Who —to contact.

Where—the offices are physically located.

Who —to contact.

Where—the offices are physically located.

| When —appointments with attorney, accountant, insurance agent are scheduled. | When —appointments with attorney, accountant, insurance agent are scheduled. |

SOS does not replace the need for legal and other professional services

In settling the business and personal affairs of the deceased, the services of attorneys, public accountants, and life underwriters are required in resolving legal matters, fulfilling accounting requirements, and in settling life insurance claims. Under no circumstances will an SOS advisor attempt to provide legal, accounting, or other professional counseling.

To assist families, SOS advisors will discuss with them areas in which the services of professionals are required and appraise them of the detailed information that will be needed to proceed directly with professional counseling. This is included in the comprehensive checklist which gives a methodical review of all possible benefits and the documents and data that will be required.

SOS pre-need booklets

For those wishing to prepare in advance for the eventual settling of business and personal affairs, the SOS bank offers a free SOS Record of Personal Information booklet in which vital data that will be required can be entered now—while all members of the family are able to contribute calmly to organizing the details that sooner or later must be faced. The booklets are available from SOS advisors. An SOS Record of Household Items is also available for the asking.

SOS is a courtesy service

You can obtain SOS assistance, an exclusive service of the SOS bank, simply by asking for it. You do not have to be a customer of the bank. The service is free and available to anyone who needs it. If a friend or relative should die in another city, you may call your SOS bank and they will give you the name of the SOS bank in that city.

SOS has compiled a list of things to do after a death has occurred.

This list has been compiled as a guide

and aid for a person who suddenly finds herself or himself in a position of responsibility after a death occurs. Everyone wants to share the burden of the people involved but usually feels helpless as to how to proceed.

Because many deaths occur between midnight and dawn, the first ten items can be taken care of in deference to the things that must wait until the daytime hours.

1. Notify proper person in the family's church.
2. Make necessary telephone calls, where travel time may be a factor.
3. Arrange for someone to spend the night with the family and give medication if prescribed by the doctor.
4. Answer and keep list of late telephone calls and/or visitors.
5. Assume responsibility for small children and arrange for them to be taken care of outside the home for a day or two (if the family so desires).
6. Check food supplies at the residence and make a grocery list (keeping in mind that food will be brought in by friends and neighbors, and probably large quantities of coffee and tissues

will be needed and should be anticipated).

7. Arrange for someone to keep a careful record of calls, food, offers of assistance, and other details.

8. Ascertain condition of clothing to be needed. (Some washing and ironing may be indicated.)

9. Select clothing to be worn by deceased and take to funeral home.

10. Help select the pallbearers and gather information that will be needed by the funeral director for the obituary.

11. Check with SOS advisor and attorney who drew the will for any special funeral instructions.

12. Determine which relatives are to stay in the home—some guestroom preparation may be necessary.

13. Make additional telephone calls to family and friends. Keep a list of all calls made and their response.

14. Schedule the appointment with the funeral director.

15. Notify employer (employees, if deceased was employer).

16. Arrange to have someone remain at the residence and straighten up during the funeral.

17. Arrange for a meeting with the attorney and insurance agent.
18. Locate all papers pertaining to the deceased, such as the will, insurance policies, and other documents. Do not throw away any papers until it has been determined by the SOS advisor that they are worthless.
19. Schedule appointment with SOS advisor for complete organization and direction.

What can I say to someone in grief?

In every grief situation, you have heard many people, one by one, say, "If there is anything I can do, let me know." The persons who make this offer mean well but it is such a shallow communication effort. Most bereaved people will not pick up the telephone and say, "I take you up on your offer. Here is something you can do."

It would be interesting if we could know what Adam said to Eve and what she said to him on the day of Abel's funeral. A deeper question would be, What did they say to each other a day later, a month later, a year later, and even a decade later? Somehow they coped in dealing with the death of their son. Since then mortal generations have been trying to cope with grief.

In many ways, what you do not say is just as important as what you do say. The following are several negative cliche's that people should avoid saying:

1. "I know just how you feel." No, you do not! You know how you felt in a similar situation, but you do not know how another person feels. You are motivated by kindness, but if you say those words you may cause alienation and uncomfortable feelings. Every grief is a new and private grief. Do not assume or presume. If there is similarity in the grief you have experienced, let the one who is currently grieving be the one to mention or claim your wisdom.

2. "How are you?" This social greeting is usually considered surface. When it is asked of a person who is deeply grieving, it is like a buzz saw cutting into his or her emotions. If the bereaved person were honest, he or she would probably reply to the question by saying "Oh, quite devastated by my loss, thank you." If you truly desire to know how people feel, listen to them.

3. "Time will heal." This is the truth. It will. It does. Yet, do not say this to the rawness of new sorrow. When you say this you are implying that the deceased will not always be as important to you as he or she is right now. The person will probably feel

like screaming back, "Do not say that! It may be true, but it adds agony now."

4. "I pity you in this situation." The grieving do not want your pity! Love, compassion, and understanding are what they desire. But not pity. Your pity will probably induce self-pity for the bereaved. This will wilt the spirit of the person.

5. "If there is anything I can do." The sorrowing person can not usually analyze enough to give correct responses to that statement. Your appropriate action would be to analyze the situation and determine what needs to be done. Then offer to do the specifics that you know you are capable of assuming. You take the initiative. Do not ask hollow questions. Get on with the business of taking care of immediate needs.

After revealing the negative communication responses to someone who is grieving, attention is shifted to what you should do. The following are some suggestions that will be positive and meaningful:

1. Take some initiatives. Do not wait to be asked to help. Look around, analyze the situation. Determine what you can do to assist immediately and ultimately and do them!

2. Listen to the grieving. Perhaps this is the most important thing you can do. During the total grief process—from beginning through readjustment—listen, listen, listen! Listen without heavy advising or lecturing. Listen with quiet inquiries at appropriate times. One of my friends put it this way when he said, "Grief wants to be heard." It not only wants to be heard, it needs to be heard. A great deal of theological and philosophical reevaluation needs to be heard from most grieving people. Above all, be a long-term listener. Listen on the first day, through the first six months, and even after a year. Do not be afraid of your silence as you listen to a bereaved person.

3. Say what you deeply feel when it is appropriate. Many people who seek to give comfort are timid in saying what they deeply feel. Be honest and simple in your statements and they will be genuinely appreciated. It is not only important to say it person to person but also by telephone. Call frequently and affirm the grieving person. It is also very meaningful to write notes and letters periodically. Above all, communicate what you are feeling!

4. Keep in touch. The expressions such as flowers, cards, and food are most appre-

ciated at first. But later on, most people tend to get too busy and forget the grieving. The rememberings later on may be even more helpful and healing than your initial contacts.

One of the most profound things that you can do for a person in sorrow is to be with him or her and communicate an attitude of your continued caring.

I do not remember much that was said to me when I was in deep sorrow, but I do remember who came to be with me during that time and even stayed in contact through grief. It is important that you do not say anything negative or disrespectful. The most important thing to do is communicate in your own way so that you care for them in their time of hurt. One of the meaningful notes that I have received was from a student in one of my classes who lost his father. The notes simply read, "Your attitude of 'I care' was a deep comfort to me."

How do I tell children about death?

Sooner or later you will be in the position of needing to communicate with a child about death. Adults can be most beneficial in aiding children in understanding life and death. Many times when adults are experiencing distress because of the death of someone, they try to protect children from knowledge and experiences about death. Death should be viewed as a family crisis time that is shared by all members of the family.

Grief is a process in which the family shares in a series of thoughts, feelings, and actions during a period of adjustment to the loss of a loved one. Therefore, in order to help children, the parents and friends must communicate ideas that are rational and helpful. A child should not be told in detail the things that he or she cannot understand. Rather than being evasive, modify the explanations to the child's level of understanding. But parents should answer children's questions about death directly and honestly.

The first exposure most children have to the words *dead* and *killed* are probably through television. These early times do not prepare them for the reality of personal loss. The parent who is wise will gently and objectively discuss death before a family loss. The discovery of dying plants or a dead pet may provide opportunity for elementary death education.

Children's reaction or response to death is usually influenced by at least three major factors: the family structure, the circumstances of the death, and the religious beliefs of the family. If the family stays together and deals with grief successfully, the children will be able to cope better with their loss and confused bewilderment.

Although many adults have good intentions, some explanations of death may cause fear, doubt, and guilt rather than comfort.

The following are some negative perspectives that should be avoided: Avoid stories and fairy tales about death. Do not give the child an explanation that you cannot accept yourself. Avoid any interpretations that may backfire and cause the child to reach conclusions that have not been intended.

Children should be told the truth. It is more disturbing for them to think that their grandmother has left them to go live with God than for them to realize that she died of a disease she did not want and fought bravely to overcome.

Many overprotective parents, in their haste to save their children from all unpleasant things, try to protect them from pain and grief. Children should not be deprived of their right to grieve. They should be free to grieve in the loss of someone they loved.

We do not have to tell all the brutal facts

but we must be honest in telling children about death. They can handle truth better than falsehoods. Children should be allowed to remain children even though they must be spoken to frankly and honestly.

When a death occurs, and children are not told the truth about what happened, they may become confused. Anxiety soon fills their minds and they fill their knowledge gap with figments of their imagination far more bizarre than the truth would be. Childhood fantasies can be carried into maturity.

In communicating with children about death, it is of paramount importance that we convey that death itself does not hurt. They must understand that the family and friends are weeping because they are sad due to the fact that they have lost a person who meant so much to them. Since children are so honest about their own feelings, then they can easily accept the adults' feelings when these feelings are adequately expressed in terms that children can comprehend.

Another major reason for being open and honest with children is that it helps adults to face their own loss. Therefore, this causes the adults to work through their own personal grief process more comfortably.

Children should never be forced to attend a funeral service, yet they should be encouraged. It can be a comforting experience for young children to go to a funeral. Therefore, they should be given a clear, detailed explanation in advance of what they can expect to see during the services. They need to know that the funeral recognizes the value and dignity of the deceased person's life. This will aid in encouraging the survivors to honestly express their feelings of disappointment and pain concerning their loss. The presence of all the family and friends at the funeral service will help children to realize that they are not alone during this time. After the funeral the children should continue to be important members of the mourners.

Since children know that death occurs, we should not try to shelter them from the normal grief process of mourning that follows. The survivors who mourn go through several stages of grief. The total grief process may include shock, weeping, panic, depression, physical distress, guilt, resentment, repression, and hope.

These complex, strong feelings and reactions to the loss of someone loved are a meaningful process in our lives. It is important to communicate to children that though we do not easily get over the loss of someone we loved, nevertheless we have to learn to live with our loss.

When sorrow is suppressed it can cause distorted or delayed grief reactions. This can cause deep psychological injury to children as well as to adults. Children need understanding when they cannot comprehend their own feelings. They must have love, acceptance, and reassurance from adults who are near them. Children should not be encouraged to hold back the flow of tears. Tears are nature's way of reducing emotional pressure and washing grief away more quickly.

Feel free to talk about past experiences involving the deceased. This will cause the deceased to become an appropriate memory for children. Then the children are more able to direct their emotions and thoughts toward the living.

Many adults need to take the word *death* off the taboo list and let it be among the concepts that are discussed openly and meaningfully. Perhaps it would help many adults to realize that some of the same principles in talking about life, sex, and birth are also appropriate in communicating about death. The following ideas may be meaningful to most adults:

1. Talk about death when children want to talk about it.
2. Determine what children are really asking.
3. It can be more devastating to answer questions that have not been asked.
4. Answers should be honest and geared to the maturation level of the child.
5. Permit the child to go through the normal grief process.

Whether you find yourself as a professional, a parent, or a friend of a child who is in sorrow, these ideas should better equip you to communicate with children concerning death. Since death is a certainty, we should not let the children be unprepared for the inevitable grief.

What is the difference in the way a Christian and non-Christian meet death?

The attitudes and words of people approaching death reveal the great difference between Christians and non-Christians. Consider these contrasts:

Francois Voltaire:

This famous French philosopher, writer, and agnostic declared in health that Christianity was a good thing for chambermaids and tailors to believe in, but not for people of wisdom. Before dying, he cried to his doctor, "I am abandoned by God and man! I will give you half of what I am worth if you will give me six month's life. Then I shall go to hell, and you will go with me. O Christ! O Jesus Christ!"

John Wesley:

The founder of Methodism is credited with redirecting England from moral disintegration while Voltaire was spreading his infamous doctrines across the Channel. He traveled a quarter of a million miles on horseback and preached 42,000 sermons. When he lay dying at the age of eighty-eight, he said confidently, "The best of all is, God is with us."

Napoleon Bonaparte:

This brilliant military strategist won many battles before being decisively defeated at the Battle of Waterloo. Later, while waiting to die, he wailed, "I die before my time, and my body will be given back to the earth. Such is the fate of him who has been called the great Napoleon. What an abyss between my deep misery and the eternal kingdom of Christ."

Ann Judson:

She arrived in Burma as a missionary two years before Napoleon's defeat at Waterloo. She and her husband, Adoniram, toiled seven years before seeing their first convert. Then Adoniram was imprisoned and tortured by the Burmese king. Ann died a short time after his release. She greeted death with these words: "Oh, the happy day will soon come when we shall meet all our friends who are now scattered—meet to part no more in our Heavenly Father's house."

Paul of Tarsus:

When Paul realized that he would soon die, he told Timothy these words: "But watch thou in all things, endure afflictions, do the work of an evangelist, make full proof of thy ministry. For I am now ready to be offered, and the time of my departure is at hand. I have fought a good fight, I have finished my course, I have kept the faith: Henceforth there is laid up for me a crown of righteousness, which the Lord, the righteous judge, shall give me at that day; and not to me only, but unto all them also that love his appearing.

How can I prepare for my own death?

Every time you go to a funeral or are associated with a death, you probably have some direct and indirect thoughts like, Someday I am going to die. . . . Someday that will be me. Then you are forced to come to grips with your feelings and fears about your own death. It is normal to feel anxious about our own future death.

Death is not necessarily a symbolic gate through which we exit this life on earth. It is an event for which we must be prepared. How are you directly or indirectly preparing for death? The question is not, How are you preparing for your loved ones' deaths? but, How are you preparing for your own?

We are going to be dead a lot longer than we will be alive on earth, so we had better plan toward eternity. Life must be more than waiting to die. It must be more than just existing on earth. Life is for living!

When I think about my own death, I consider several areas that help me to evaluate how well I am prepared for my death date. I invite you to evaluate these areas:

1. Are you living in a right relationship with God? Have you commited yourself to God in terms of Saviorship and Lordship?

2. Are you living in right relationship with your family, friends, and associates? Are there any relationships that need reconciliation and repair? Have you learned to disagree without being disagreeable? Are you enjoying people?
3. Are you investing your life in things that will last for eternity, or have you commited your life to things that will perish when you die?

One day you will have to face your own death. There is so much that you can do to prepare for it. Now is the time to settle these matters and make your preparations.

Where can I find help in the Bible when I have a time of need?

These quick references in scripture will be a significant aid in helping you find resolutions to many of the needs that you may have while in the grief process.

When you are facing grief:
>   Romans 8:26-28
>   Philippians 1:21
>   2 Corinthians 1:3-5
>   2 Corinthians 5:8

When you have lost your sense of worth,

value, and dignity:
>Psalm 139

When you are feeling inadequate and weak:
>2 Corinthians 12:9-10
>Philippians 4:13

When you are feeling depressed and lonely:
>Psalm 23
>Romans 8
>Hebrews 13:5

When you are in need of forgiveness:
>Hebrews 4:15-16
>1 John 1:9

When you want to be controlled by the Holy Spirit:
>Psalm 106:13-15
>Philippians 4:8
>1 John 2:15-17

When seeking inner serenity and peace during a time of turmoil:
>Isaiah 26:3
>John 14:27
>John 16:33
>Philippians 4:6-7

When you need to conquer your fears:
Psalm 27:1
2 Timothy 1:7

When you need courage:
Psalm 138:3
Ephesians 6:10-13

When you are suffering afflictions:
Psalm 34:19
2 Corinthians 4:17
1 Peter 4:12-13
1 Peter 5:10

When your patience is being tried:
Romans 8:28-29
James 1:2-4

When you are facing temptations, decision making, and need wisdom:
1 Corinthians 10:13
James 1:2-6
James 1:12-15

When you desire guidance:
Proverbs 3:5-6
James 1:5

When your problems are getting you down:

Psalm 55:22
1 Peter 5:7

When you are tired, weary, and in need of strength and rest:
Isaiah 40:28-31
Matthew 11:28-30
Galatians 6:9

When you feel that you are being treated unjustly:
1 Peter 2:19-23
1 Peter 4:12-15

When you are facing failure:
Romans 8:28-29

When you are facing danger and needing protection:
Psalm 23
Psalm 91
Psalm 121

When you have doubts about your salvation:
John 3:16
Romans 10:9-10
1 John 5:11-13

When you have doubts about God's keep-

ing power:
> Romans 8:38-39
> Philippians 1:6
> 1 Peter 1:5

When you desire provisions for life's basic needs:
> Matthew 6:33

When you are worried that your sharing of God's Word is of no avail:
> Isaiah 55:11

Conclusion

IN this book you have been confronted with some questions and answers about death and the grief process. Now you have several alternatives: you may choose to dwell on your grief in a morbid way; you may choose to feel sorry for yourself; you may choose to make other people miserable; or you may find a new normal life and help others because of your experience.

In your grief, you have been going through a deep experience. It has not been an experience that you wanted, but one that has resulted in painful truth about life and death. This truth has brought about the reality that we do not know how to live until we know how to die!

Grief behavior may take different forms. It may take the form of facing up to what has happened, or it may result from problems caused by the blockage of bottling-up feelings.

Expression of grief is therapeutic! These factors are extremely important:

1. Admit it! You must admit to yourself what has happened in the death situation. Boldly say aloud to yourself, "My loved one is dead because of a fatal disease." In other words, call them by name and admit why they are dead.
2. Vent it! After you have admitted to yourself why your loved one died, then tell others how you feel about your loss. Get your feelings out. I encourage you to talk, cry, scream—just get your deep emotional feelings out of your system.
3. Release it! After you have admitted to yourself and others how you feel about your loss, then release your feelings. To release your feelings means to open up and turn them over to God. Then release your loved one. Give them permission to be with God until you join them. Also give yourself permission to enjoy living on earth until you join God and your loved one!

How do you help someone in the grief

process? Perhaps you telephone, go to see them, send flowers or money to a meaningful cause, invite them over to your home once or twice to prove that you care, and then you slip back into your own routine life assuring yourself that you have done all that anyone could do. That is not enough! Persons in grief need you desperately. To help them effectively demands an understanding of the grief process, a willingness to listen and a lot of time. Become involved in their life and help with any areas in which they may need assistance. Most of all, be a genuine friend who communicates that you care. Most of the time the funeral is not the end of the grief process; it is only the beginning.

In the process of learning how to live and die are certain factors about our behavior that are frightening but normal. If we treat our normal feelings of grief as if they were abnormal, our mind short circuits; thus, guilt and frustration result. We must treat normal human feelings normally!

Most important, you may find power in the Christian faith that you did not realize was there until you put Scripture to work in your life. Through the Word of God you will find a faith stronger than death! Because you now have some deeper insights into the normal grief process, you will be better able to communicate with a person in grief.

Definition of Terms

Christian
: A person who has an established relationship with God through his Son, Jesus Christ (Rom. 10:9-10; John 3:16; 1 Tim. 2:5-6).

Death
: Physical death—Separation (transition) of body and spirit, resulting in decay of the body (Eccles. 12:7).

  Spirit death—Separation of the spirit from God, resulting in the ruin of the spirit (2 Thess. 1:8-9).

Defense mechanism
: A reaction designed to protect an individual's self-image of adequacy and worth rather than to acknowledge and cope directly with the stress and

91

sorrow situation.

Depression   Emotional state of dejection
             or despair and feelings of
             worthlessness and apprehen-
             sion; a profound feeling of
             sadness and sorrow.

Emotion   Expression of one's deep feel-
             ings. Emotions cannot be sep-
             arated from situations or ex-
             periences that evoke them.
             Emotion is an inside ther-
             mometer that is affected by
             outside events.

Empathy   Ability to understand and to
             some extent share the state of
             experiences (mental, physical,
             emotional, spiritual) of another
             person.

Faith   Confidence in God and his
             ability to guide and provide
             for the individual's needs (Heb.
             11:1-6).

God's Word   God's thoughts revealed to the
             human race through the Bible.
             The revelation of God's actions
             with his people throughout the
             ages, particularly through his

Son, Jesus Christ (2 Tim. 3:16).

Grief Process (Death)	A series of thoughts, feelings, and actions during a period of adjustment to the loss of a loved one.
Guilt	A feeling of having committed a breach of conduct. Guilt comes when one does not meet what he or she expects of himself or herself as well as what others expect of him or her.
Heaven	Eternal presence with the Lord God. The final dwelling place of the Christian is known as heaven (John 14:2-3, Rev. 21:4).
Hell	Eternal absence from the Lord God. The final dwelling place of the non-Christian is called hell (Mark 9:48).
Hope	An expectation toward attaining an equilibrium in that all things work together for good for those who love the Lord and are trying to fulfill his purposes (Romans 8:28).

Life	Physical life (life before death). The period of duration of a person in the earthly physical body. Spirit life (life after death). The life in which a Christian is absent from the body and present with the Lord God.
Panic	Sudden severe overpowering fright involving intense anxiety.
Pray	Communication with God. The offering of adoration, confession, thanksgiving, and supplication to God (John 16:24).
Repression	Means by which intolerable memories are kept out of the consciousness.
Resentment	The feeling of indignant displeasure because of something regarded as wrong.
Shock	A blow, impact, sudden agitation of the mental or emotional senses.
Sin	Anything according to Scripture that interferes with an

adequate relationship with God through his Son, Jesus Christ.

Sorrow   Mental and emotional suffering or sadness that arises from the loss of a loved one.

Sympathy   An association or relationship between people so that whatever affects one similarly affects the other or others. Sympathy emphasizes pity rather than awareness of the state of another person.

Trust   Assured reliance on God with confident hope (Heb. 11).

Suggested Readings

Bayly, Joseph. *The View From a Hearse.* Elgin, Ill.: David C. Cook, 1969.

Billheimer, Paul. *Don't Waste Your Sorrows.* Ft. Washington, Pa.: Christian Literature Crusade, 1977.

Jackson, Edgar. *Understanding Grief: Its Roots, Dynamics and Treatment.* New York: Abingdon Press, 1957.

Kubler-Ross, Elizabeth. *On Death and Dying.* New York: Macmillan, Inc., 1970.

Lewis, C.S. *A Grief Observed.* New York: Seabury Press, 1961.

Lewis, C.S. *Mere Christianity.* New York: Macmillan Inc., 1960.

Oates, Wayne. *Your Particular Grief.* Philadelphia: The Westminster Press, 1981.

Phillips, J.B. *Your God Is Too Small.* New York: Macmillan Inc., 1961.

Tanner, Ira J. *The Gift of Grief.* New York: Hawthorne, 1976.

Westburg, Granger. *Good Grief: A Constructive Approach to the Problem of Loss.* Philadelphia: Fortress Press, 1972.